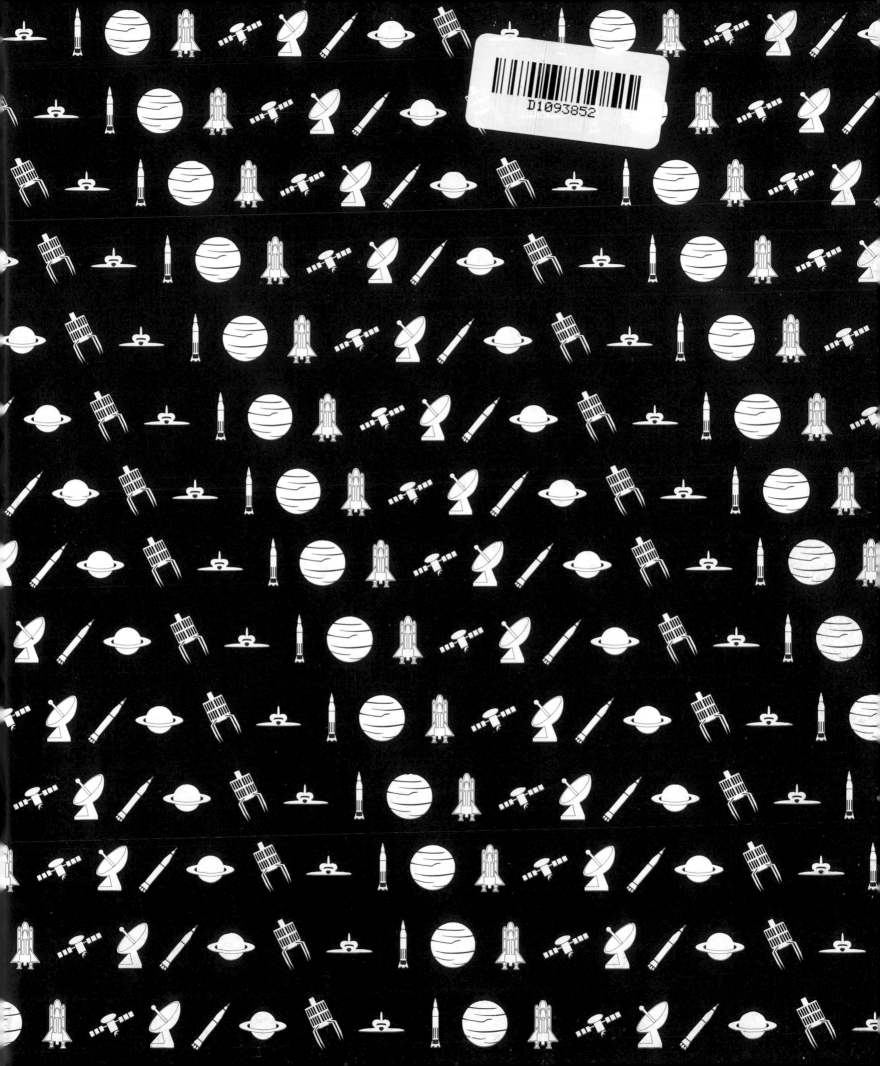

FOREWORD

"Reading through the pages of this book caused me to think about the great fun of making a spaceflight. I well remember the bone-rattling lift-off, the rocket's push accelerating us beyond the edge of the Earth, the sudden silence of these same engines as they shut down, and then the eerie quiet of coasting in unending orbit around our beautiful planet. I hope you enjoy reading this book as much as I have."

Joe (Joseph) Allen
Mission specialist on Space Shuttle missions STS-5 and 51-A.

ACKNOWLEDGMENTS

The author and publisher would like to thank Joe Allen, president of Space Industries International; Dave Portree and many others at the various NASA facilities; Neville Kidger; Andy Salmon and Mike Shayler, for their assistance in the preparation of *Exploring Space;* and the following individuals and organizations for their kind permission to reproduce the photographs used in this book:

Boeing: 32 bottom left. Britstock-IFA Ltd: 11 top. Genesis Space Photo Library: 27 top (NASA), 31 top right. Michael Holford: 4. Neville Kidger: 40 center. Kobal Collection: 6 left. NASA: 9 bottom, 10, 14, 21 bottom, 21 top, 24 left, 26, 27 bottom, 28 top, 29 left, 29 top right, 32 top, 32 center right, 34 bottom left, 39. Novosti: 40 bottom left. Quadrant Picture Library: 13 right, 24 right (NASA). Scala (Museo della Scienza, Firenze): 5 bottom left. Science Photo Library: 5 top (Roger Ressmeyer, Starlight), 5 bottom right (Chris Butler), 7 bottom left (NASA), 8 left (NASA), 9 top (Novosti), 15 bottom (R. Ressmeyer, Starlight), 16 bottom (NASA), 22 center (R. Ressmeyer, Starlight), 28 center (NASA), 28 bottom (R. Ressmeyer, Starlight), 29 center (NASA), 30-31 (NASA), 34 bottom right (Tony Ward, Tetbury), 44 (R. Ressmeyer, Starlight), 45 (David Hardy). Space Commerce Corporation: 40 top right. Starland Picture Library: 11 bottom left (NASA), 13 left (ESA), 29 bottom right (NASA). TASS: 20. Telegraph Colour Library: 18, 37. Topham Picture Source: 6 right, 15 top (AP), 38.

ILLUSTRATORS

Arcana: 8, 9, 15, 20, 44 bottom right, 46-47. Peter Bull: 12 top, 14. Joe Lawrence: 30, 34-35, 36, 37, 38-39, 44 top right, 45 top left. Maltings Partnership: 4-5, 6-7, 7, 10, 11, 12 bottom, 16, 17, 20-21, 22-23, 24, 25, 26-27, 33, 41, 42-43, 45 bottom. Brian MacIntyre: 18-19. Ed Stuart: 6 bottom left and right, 31, 35, 39 bottom, 42.

First American edition, 1994

Library of Congress Cataloging-in-Publication Data
Shayler, David.
Space / David Shayler. — 1st American ed.
p. cm.
Includes index.
1. Astronautics — Juvenile literature   [Astronautics.]   I. Title.
TL793.S429   1994   94-7755
629.4—dc20
ISBN 0-679-84920-3

Manufactured by Proost, Belgium.
1 2 3 4 5 6 7 8 9 10

CONTENTS

WATCHING THE SKIES **4**

INTO SPACE **6**

THE RIGHT STUFF **8**

TO THE MOON **10**

LAUNCHERS **12**

THE SPACE BASES **14**

LIFT-OFF! **16**

A *SOYUZ* LAUNCH

A JOURNEY THROUGH SPACE **18**

RETURN TO EARTH **20**

GROUND CONTROL **22**

SPACE SHUTTLE **24**

THE ORBITER

ORBITAL OPERATIONS **26**

LIFE IN SPACE **28**

MADE IN SPACE **30**

SPACESUITS **32**

SPACESUITS

EYE IN THE SKY **34**

SPACE PROBES **36**

SPACE STATIONS **38**

SPACE STATION *MIR* **40**

THE *MIR* ACHIEVEMENT

TO THE PLANETS **42**

FUTURE DEVELOPMENTS **44**

SPACE LOG **46**

INDEX **48**

WATCHING THE SKIES

People have watched the skies from the earliest times. The objects most easily seen were the Sun and Moon. They were worshipped as gods and goddesses, and became part of myths and legends.

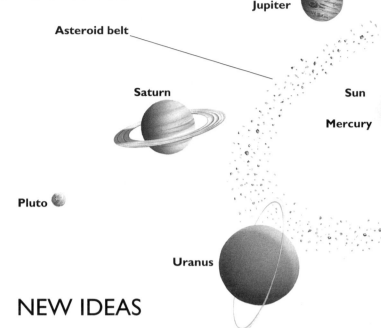

Jupiter

Asteroid belt

Saturn

Sun

Mercury

Pluto

Uranus

ASTROLOGY

The stars and planets, too, were part of the mysterious world beyond the reach of humans. The movements of these "heavenly bodies" seemed to announce important events, such as the start of spring, or a time of floods. Many people believed the stars and planets controlled all events on Earth. Some people, called astrologers, tried to predict the future by studying the skies.

In ancient Greece, the astronomer Aristarchus figured out that these stars and planets did not travel around the Earth, but that the Earth moved in the sky. Most people did not believe him. For over a thousand years most people believed the Earth was the center of the Universe. Everything else - the "heavenly bodies" - was placed there by God to service the needs of the Earth and Man.

NEW IDEAS

During the Renaissance - a "rebirth" of learning from the 14th to the 17th centuries - scholars rediscovered the ideas of Aristarchus. Astronomers such as Copernicus in Poland, Galileo in Italy, and Newton in England worked out the movements of the Earth and other planets. They found that all of them revolved around, or circled, the Sun. This work laid the foundations for the logical, scientific study of the Universe.

The passing of a comet, probably Halley's Comet, is recorded in the Bayeux tapestry (right), believed to be from the 11th or 12th century. Over 2,000 years ago, the ancient Chinese and Egyptians charted the movements of the planets out to Saturn. The outer planets of our solar system were discovered many years later: Uranus in 1781, Neptune in 1846, and Pluto in 1930.

ISTIMIRANT STELLA

HAROLD

This is how our solar system might look from a space probe leaving the system - though the planets would be much smaller, and millions of miles apart. All of the planets orbit, or circle, the Sun.

Mars

Moon

Earth

Venus

Neptune

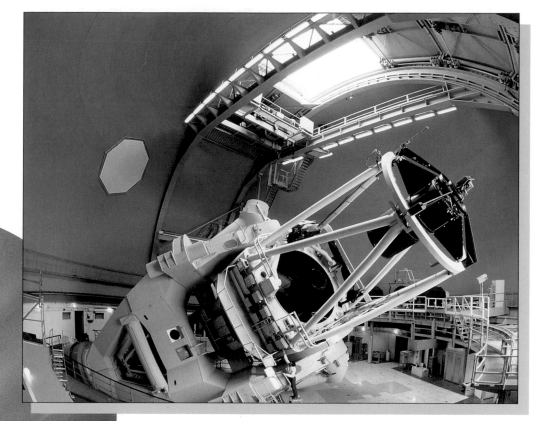

Telescopes like this have shown that our solar system is part of a cluster of 100 billion stars, called a galaxy. There are millions of galaxies in the Universe.

The Universe is a huge place. It is so big that scientists measure very big distances in "light years" - the distance light travels in a year, about 5,900,000,000,000 miles. Here are a few distances.

Earth to Moon: 240,000 miles
Earth to Sun: 93,000,000 miles
Width of our solar system: 6,200,000,000 miles
Distance to the next closest galaxy:
1,000,000,000,000,000,000 miles

This is the type of telescope perfected by the Italian astronomer Galileo Galilei at the beginning of the 17th century. It enabled Galileo to make new discoveries about the solar system - the planets orbiting our Sun.

TVBVM OPTICVM VIDES GALILAEI INVENTVM ET OPVS, QVO SOLIS MACVLAS
ET EXIMOS LVNAE MONTES, ET IOVIS SATELLITES, ET NOVAM QVASI
RERVM VNIVERSITATE PRIMVS DISPEXIT A. MDCIX.

◆ INTO SPACE

At the same time as the science of astronomy was being developed, people were speculating about what the stars and planets were like. The next stage was to actually go into space and study them.

ROCKETRY

In the 20th century, the new technology of rocketry was developed. In Russia, Konstantin Tsiolkovsky provided the theory of spaceflight and forecast the use of spacesuits, rockets, and space stations, half a century before the space age began. In Germany, Hermann Oberth worked on the early theories of rockets and space travel. Then, in 1926, American Robert Goddard put theory into practice by launching the world's first successful liquid-fueled rocket. These "fathers of spaceflight" had showed the way for humans to escape the pull of Earth's gravity and to travel beyond the Earth.

In the 1950s a series of experimental aircraft were developed, such as the X-15 shown here. Launched at high altitude, they ignited their rocket engines and climbed to around 50 miles, the boundary of air and space. They landed on a runway, similarly to the Space Shuttle today.

The invention of movies in the early half of this century led to many ideas about space travel and bug-eyed monsters. Above is one film-maker's idea of a Moon landing, and on the right is a possible insectoid visitor from space.

In the 1930s, scientists tried to reach the outer atmosphere using capsules lifted by balloons (top). Russia's Sputnik 1 (above) was the world's first artificial satellite. Only 1 foot in diameter, it sent a few simple signals back to Earth. Sputnik 2 (right) carried the first living creature into orbit - a dog named Laika.

POSTWAR PROGRESS

During World War II, Germany developed missile and rocket technology for military uses. After the war, many of the scientists continued their research in the Soviet Union and the United States. The Soviet Union launched its first intercontinental ballistic missile (ICBM), a long-range, guidable missile, in 1955. Then, on October 4, 1957, an ICBM was used to put *Sputnik 1*, the world's first satellite, into orbit around the Earth. In the United States, the Navy's *Vanguard 1* and the Army's *Explorer 1* competed to be the first U.S. satellite. On January 31, 1958, *Explorer 1* was orbited. The space age was now a space race.

American pioneer Robert Goddard stands by his historic liquid-fueled rocket, first launched on March 16, 1926. Exactly 40 years later Neil Armstrong, the first human on the Moon, made his first spaceflight.

In the 19th century, writer Jules Verne described this "spacetrain." Even then it was believed that journeys into space would become everyday events.

U.S AIR FORCE

THE RIGHT STUFF

On April 12, 1961, Soviet cosmonaut Yuri Gagarin became the first person to travel into space. He orbited the Earth in 108 minutes in his spacecraft, *Vostok 1*, beginning a new method of exploration - manned spaceflight.

SPACE EXPLORERS

Since then, over 300 people have flown in space. In the 1950s, no one knew how the stress of launch, weightlessness, and reentry into the atmosphere would affect the human body. Therefore military test pilots were chosen to be the first space travelers. It was thought that their physical fitness, flying skill, and experience of pushing high-performance aircraft to the very limits would enable them to withstand the stress of flying in a spacecraft.

PIONEERS

The first astronauts were pioneering explorers risking their lives to increase our knowledge of space. Now that the effects of space travel are known, astronauts no longer need to be pilots, but rather, scientists. As space stations are built, the roles of engineers, technicians, and researchers become even more important. When bases are established on the Moon and Mars, astronauts will become builders, mining engineers, and farmers, like the 19th century pioneers of the American West.

This cosmonaut is on a multi-axial trainer, which will help him get used to the disorientation of spaceflight. Astronauts spend months practicing every minute of the mission, following a timetable called a flight plan.

The first astronauts had to be the right size to fit the spacecraft! For example, the Mercury capsule (above and right) was only 7 feet high - a tight fit for an astronaut in a spacesuit.

The first person in space, Russian Yuri Gagarin (right), is shown in the cabin of Vostok 1. Vostok 1 orbited the Earth in a flight lasting 108 minutes.

The U.S. astronaut below is training for zero gravity (weightlessness) in an aircraft nicknamed the "Vomit Comet." It flies in a rollercoaster pattern; at the top of the pattern the astronauts experience zero gravity.

WHAT IS THE "RIGHT STUFF"?

Are you made of the "right stuff" to be an astronaut? There is no age limit, but you must be mentally and physically fit, and have a science degree. To be a pilot astronaut - qualified to fly the spacecraft - you must have 1,000 hours on high-performance jet aircraft. If you just have a scientific background you can still be a mission specialist, carrying out research. Other scientists can also train for a short time to carry out specialist research in space.

TO THE MOON

Even before the first satellites were put into space, there were plans to send machines called probes to the Moon and planets. In 1961, President John F. Kennedy declared that an American would land on the Moon's surface before 1970.

FIRST PROBES

The Soviet effort to reach the Moon began with its *Luna* probes. In 1959 *Luna 2* sent back photos as it approached the Moon before crash-landing on the surface; in 1966 *Luna 9* landed and sent back 27 photos; and in 1970 *Luna 16* returned with rock samples!

Some ways to visit the Moon are shown in the diagram on the right. Many of the early missions did not even get beyond Earth orbit!

3. Unmanned soft landing, (Luna 9) and return (Luna 16)

1. Fly by (Luna 1)

4. Unmanned orbit (Luna 10), manned orbit and return (Apollo 8)

5. Manned landing and return (Apollo 11)

2. Crash landing (Luna 2)

Cameras

Solar panel

Antenna

Ranger 7's six cameras sent over 4,000 pictures in 19 minutes before impact on the Moon.

Listed below are some of the 80-plus unmanned missions to the Moon. *Surveyor 3* (right), which landed in April 1967, was visited by *Apollo 12's* astronauts in November 1969.

Luna 1	USSR	01/59	**Flew by Moon**
Luna 2	USSR	09/59	**Crash-landed after taking photos**
Ranger 7	USA	07/64	**Sent back 4,300 photos**
Luna 9	USSR	01/66	**First soft landing**
Luna 10	USSR	03/66	**First probe to achieve lunar orbit**
Surveyor 1	USA	05/66	**Sent back 11,000 pictures**
Luna 13	USSR	12/66	**Tested soil**
Luna 16	USSR	09/70	**First automatic soil sample returned**
Luna 17	USSR	11/70	**First moon rover taken to surface**
Muses-A	Japan	01/90	**First to visit since 1976 (Luna 24)**

A GIANT STEP FOR MANKIND

The Americans made it to the Moon first. Despite a later start in the space race, they sent a number of probes to the Moon. Then, on July 20, 1969, the *Apollo 11* mission with Neil Armstrong and Edwin "Buzz" Aldrin landed on the surface. As the world watched this historic event, the third astronaut, Mike Collins, orbited the Moon in the command module. He even went out of radio contact with the Earth when he passed behind the Moon. Later *Apollo* astronauts gathered more samples, and drove a Lunar Rover about 10 miles from the lunar module. In all, six *Apollo* missions landed on the Moon.

Astronaut Jack Schmitt stands with the lunar module Challenger, *the* Lunar Rover, *and the U.S. flag during* Apollo 17's *mission in 1972. This was the last of six* Apollo *landings.*

Apollo 9's command module orbits Earth in March 1969. This photo was taken from the lunar module on its first test flight.

DID YOU KNOW?

Spacecraft must be as light as possible. The ladder used by Neil Armstrong to climb down onto the Moon's surface could take his weight only because of the low gravity on the Moon. It would have broken under his real weight on Earth!

The return capsule, filled with soil samples, lifts off from Luna 16 *(right).*

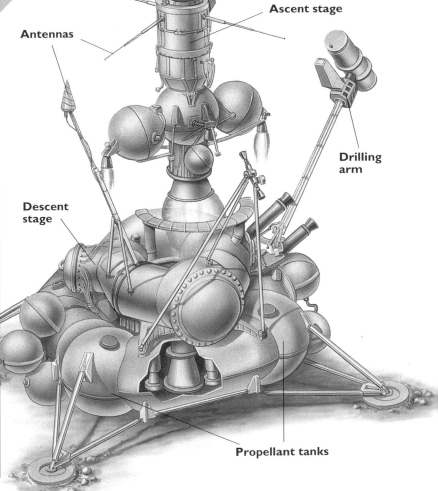

Automatic return capsule

Ascent stage

Antennas

Drilling arm

Descent stage

Propellant tanks

◆ LAUNCHERS

The rocket, first used by the Chinese over 1,000 years ago, is the only practical way to enter space. It will remain the most efficient method of putting spacecraft into space for many years to come.

ROCKETS

In a rocket engine, fuel is burned to create hot gases. The force of these gases rushing out of the exhausts pushes the rocket in the opposite direction, much the way an air-filled balloon zooms forward, if you let it go, until all the air rushes out. The larger the rocket, the more power it generates and the more weight it can carry.

Here are some of the major launchers used in the space program. The Saturn *family of rockets was developed for the* Apollo *moon program in the 1960s. Most of the 360-foot-tall Saturn V rocket was made up of the three huge stages needed to put the spacecraft on route to the Moon. Only the 12.8-foot-tall Apollo 17 reentry module holding the three astronauts was recovered at the end of the mission.*

Apollo-Saturn V

Reentry module

Less power and fuel are needed when a rocket is lighter. Therefore, rockets are made up of sections, or stages. As each stage's fuel is used up, the empty stage is jettisoned (thrown off) to lose weight (above).

Space Transportation System (Space Shuttle)

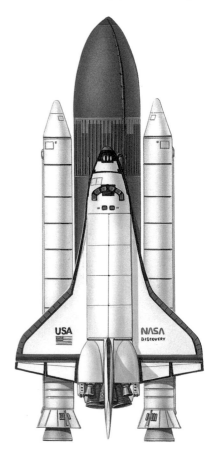

Soyuz SL-4 (Rakyeta Nosityel Soyuz)

Gemini-Titan

Mercury-Atlas

1962-63
USA

1965-66
USA

1967 to date
USSR/Russia

1968-72
manned missions
USA

1981 to date
manned missions
USA

A JOURNEY IN SPACE

A spacecraft must be able to fly at about 18,000 miles per hour to escape the pull of gravity and stay in orbit around the Earth - that's almost 100 times faster than the fastest racing car. If it flies too slowly, gravity will soon pull it back to Earth.

Many countries still use rockets to put payloads into space. The European Ariane *is one of these designs.*

DID YOU KNOW?

Rocket fuel is very explosive, so it needs special storage. It has to be kept very cold so it does not evaporate. If you could have sealed an ice cube in a *Saturn V* rocket tank, it would have taken eight years to melt!

ROCKET POWER

To reach this velocity, a spacecraft needs a very powerful engine. Even the powerful engines of airplane jets are not strong enough for spaceflight. Also, jet engines need oxygen from air in order to work, and there isn't any air in space.

The only engine that can work in space is a rocket, because it carries its own supply of oxygen as well as fuel.

Japan, India, and China have successful launchers. This artist's impression shows a Japanese H-II lift-off.

SHUTTLE SYSTEM

Most spacecraft can only be used for one mission. However, NASA's Space Shuttle system was designed to fly mission after mission. The Shuttle orbiter is launched by firing three main engines (fueled from a massive external tank) and two solid rocket boosters. Only the external tank is lost; everything else can be recovered and reused.

THE SPACE BASES

Space missions begin months, sometimes years, before the moment of launch. All the preparations come to an end when the equipment and crew are together at the launch site, ready for takeoff.

KSC

Perhaps the most famous launch site is Kennedy Space Center (KSC) in Florida. Missions are launched out across the Atlantic away from heavily populated cities.

Yuri Gagarin was launched from the Baikonur Cosmodrome in Central Asia. This huge area, over 4,500 miles square, includes several launch areas where the spacecraft are prepared for missions. All Soviet cosmonauts have taken off from here, as have several unmanned missions.

The Space Shuttle **Atlantis** *is moved to the launch pad at KSC (above).*

The major launch sites (below). Launches can be made into many different types of orbit.

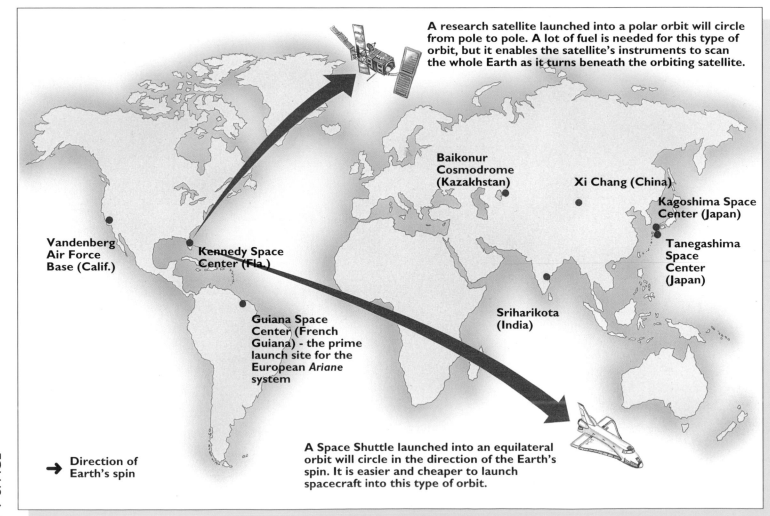

A research satellite launched into a polar orbit will circle from pole to pole. A lot of fuel is needed for this type of orbit, but it enables the satellite's instruments to scan the whole Earth as it turns beneath the orbiting satellite.

Baikonur Cosmodrome (Kazakhstan)

Xi Chang (China)

Kagoshima Space Center (Japan)

Vandenberg Air Force Base (Calif.)

Kennedy Space Center (Fla.)

Tanegashima Space Center (Japan)

Guiana Space Center (French Guiana) - the prime launch site for the European *Ariane* system

Sriharikota (India)

→ Direction of Earth's spin

A Space Shuttle launched into an equilateral orbit will circle in the direction of the Earth's spin. It is easier and cheaper to launch spacecraft into this type of orbit.

STACKING

All sections of a launch vehicle are brought to KSC for checking before being "stacked," or assembled, on the vehicle that will launch them. This vehicle is then taken to the launch pad. The whole mission is planned around a fixed deployment time or rendezvous (see page 18).

A Russian crew - actually two Russians and a Japanese cosmonaut - head for their awaiting Soyuz spacecraft. They will waddle, rather than walk, in their cumbersome spacesuits.

Away from the launch pad, equipment is being assembled. These units will eventually boost a probe into deep space.

Even at night there's activity on the launch pad. Work continues around the clock to launch in time for a set rendezvous or deployment.

READY FOR LAUNCH

Once the vehicle is on the launch pad, hundreds of computers monitor and test every one of its systems. Fuel is loaded in from huge tanks around the pad, and finally the remaining payloads are put aboard. The crew usually board the vehicle about two hours before launch, and support astronauts help them strap in. Then the hatches are sealed and the pad evacuated. The crew must now wait for launch.

◆LIFT-OFF!

The lift-off has always been the most dangerous part of any spaceflight. Sitting on top of thousands of gallons of fuel is always a risky operation. There are hundreds of things that have to work in sequence before the vehicle lifts off the pad.

LAUNCH

Seconds before launch the computers tell the engines to ignite. They burst into fire and all ground connections are severed. Clamps hold the spacecraft for a few seconds to let thrust build up, then they are released and flight begins. "Lift-off . . . We have lift-off!" calls ground control as the vehicle clears the launch tower and heads for space.

"Tower clear!" As the spacecraft climbs, atmospheric pressure on its surface increases. The Space Shuttle rolls 120° to ease this pressure on the orbiter, the airplane-like part of the vehicle.

Preparations for the next launch begin immediately after touchdown. Below, a huge crane lifts the Shuttle's orbiter onto a carrier aircraft. The orbiter will be taken to KSC for more processing, and its next lift-off.

"GO AT THROTTLE UP!"

As the vehicle climbs, empty stages detach and the speed increases. As engines burn out and stages separate, the crew experience a short lunge forward as the momentum of flight slows, then they're kicked back into their seats as the new engines ignite.

A BUMPY RIDE

There is not much the crew can do as computers tick away the planned sequence of events. Inside it's a very bumpy ride as the crew are pressed into their seats due to the G-forces caused by the great acceleration at launch. Finally the spacecraft separates from the last stage and fires a small control jet to punch it into a safe orbit 100 miles above the Earth. The most dangerous part is over.

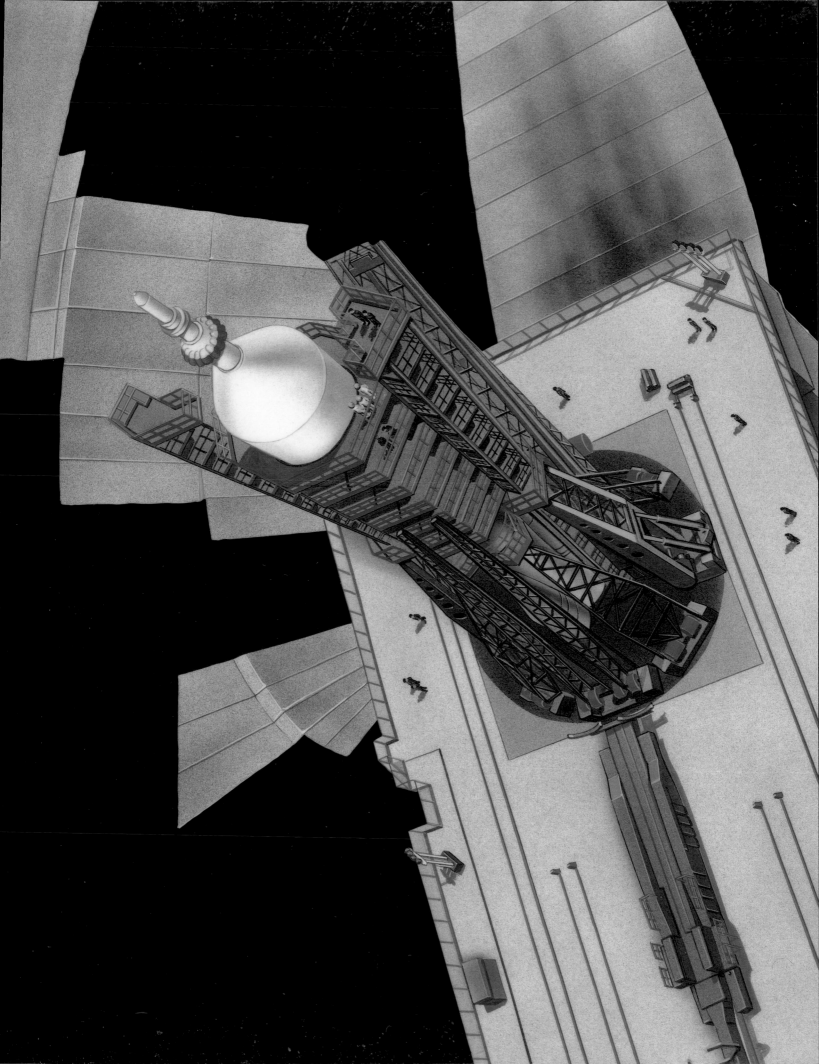

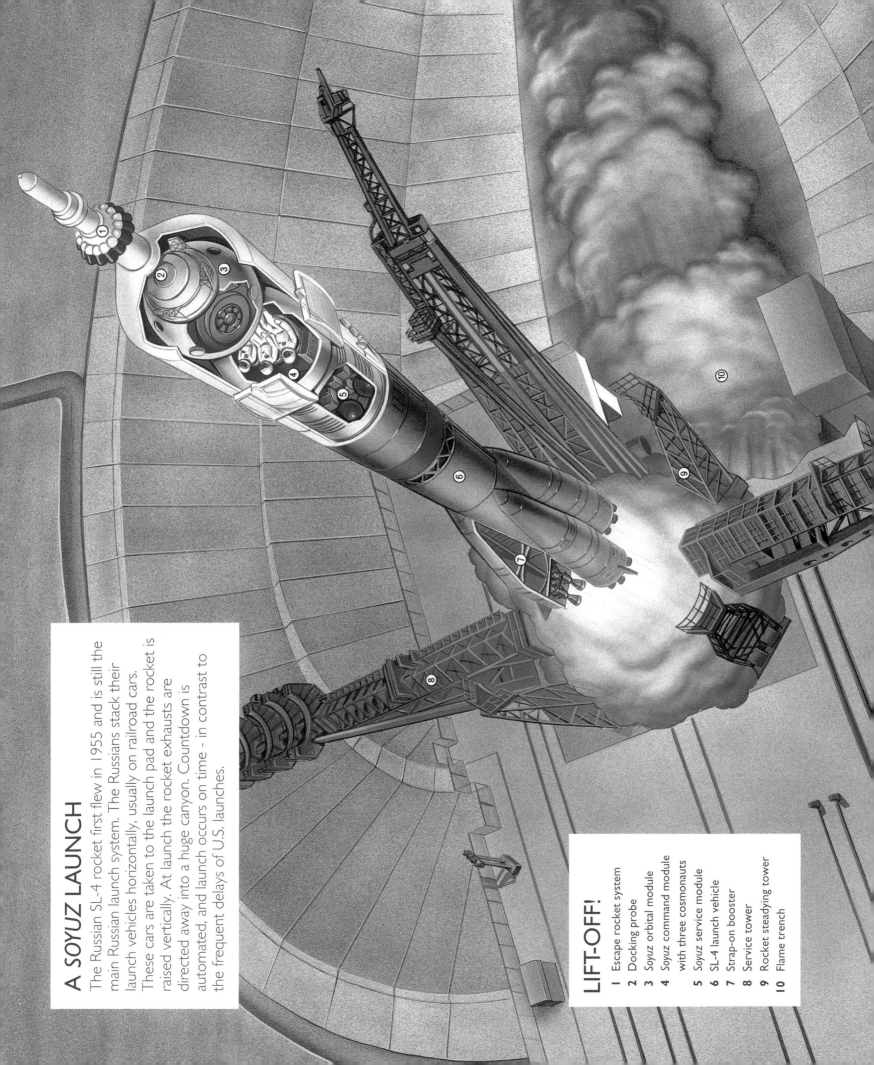

A SOYUZ LAUNCH

The Russian SL-4 rocket first flew in 1955 and is still the main Russian launch system. The Russians stack their launch vehicles horizontally, usually on railroad cars. These cars are taken to the launch pad and the rocket is raised vertically. At launch the rocket exhausts are directed away into a huge canyon. Countdown is automated, and launch occurs on time - in contrast to the frequent delays of U.S. launches.

LIFT-OFF!

1 Escape rocket system
2 Docking probe
3 Soyuz orbital module
4 Soyuz command module
   with three cosmonauts
5 Soyuz service module
6 SL-4 launch vehicle
7 Strap-on booster
8 Service tower
9 Rocket steadying tower
10 Flame trench

A JOURNEY THROUGH SPACE

Every spacecraft is launched to perform a mission. This might be to deploy (put into position) a satellite, to rendezvous (meet up) with another spacecraft, or to visit a distant planet. Scientists must calculate the launch time and flight path of the mission carefully.

RIGHT TIME, RIGHT PATH

The Earth, the planets, and other spacecraft all move in regular patterns in space. Therefore there are only certain times, called launch windows, when a spacecraft can be launched to meet its target. If a launch misses its window, it must wait for another one, which may be days or even months away.

Once in space, the spacecraft must be navigated (steered). On the Space Shuttle, the crew take visual sightings of certain stars and planets. Their computer compares these sightings with its own data, and calculates the Shuttle's true position.

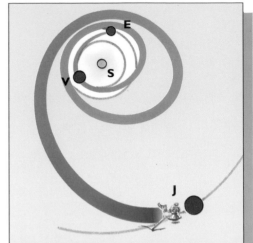

The *Galileo* space probe was launched toward the Sun (S). It used the gravity of Venus (V) and the Earth (E) to propel it like a slingshot on its six-year journey to Jupiter (J).

Lift-off! A rocket burns lots of fuel. To lift one ton of payload (equipment) into orbit, a rocket needs five tons of fuel. However, a spacecraft needs fuel only to escape from a planet's gravity, or to change course.

A HELPING HAND

The space probe *Galileo* was launched on a mission to Jupiter. It was taken into space by the Space Shuttle, then fired on its way by a special booster. When the booster used up its fuel, it detached, leaving *Galileo* with just enough fuel for maneuvering.

SLINGSHOT

Galileo was actually launched toward the sun! Scientists calculated its journey so that *Galileo* could use the gravity of other planets to swing it farther on its way. This "slingshot" effect is like a person leaping on a fast-moving carousel and then jumping off, but now moving even faster! Using this effect meant that most of *Galileo*'s payload could be scientific equipment, not fuel.

Six months before Galileo reaches Jupiter, it will launch an entry probe. When the probe enters the planet's atmosphere, it will release a parachute to slow its fall. This will give it more time to send data before being destroyed by Jupiter's violent, stormy atmosphere.

Galileo's entry probe can be carried in the engine outlet because the main booster is needed only to steer the main probe into orbit around Jupiter. However, Galileo must keep its communications antenna pointing at Earth. It maneuvers using small rockets called thrusters.

A moving craft in space doesn't need to keep its engine on because there's no air to slow it down. To go faster it fires its engine just long enough to reach the correct speed. To slow down, however, a spacecraft can't put its brakes on! First, it has to turn to face in the opposite direction. It does this by firing small rockets on its side, called thrusters. When it has turned around, the main engine can then be fired against the direction of flight, to slow the spacecraft.

Direction of flight

Direction of flight

RETURN TO EARTH

Returning to Earth is nearly as difficult as takeoff. The reentry module has to fly through the atmosphere. And the high speed of reentry will generate very high temperatures on the outside of the craft.

RESISTING THE HEAT

Before reentry, the crew fire the engines against the direction of flight, to slow down. They then separate the reentry module from the rest of the spacecraft. Special tiles protect the module from the incredible heat generated when it reenters Earth's atmosphere. The heat is caused by friction, as air rubs against the speeding craft.

Survival courses prepare astronauts for emergencies. In 1965, two cosmonauts spent 24 hours in the wilderness waiting for the rescue team.

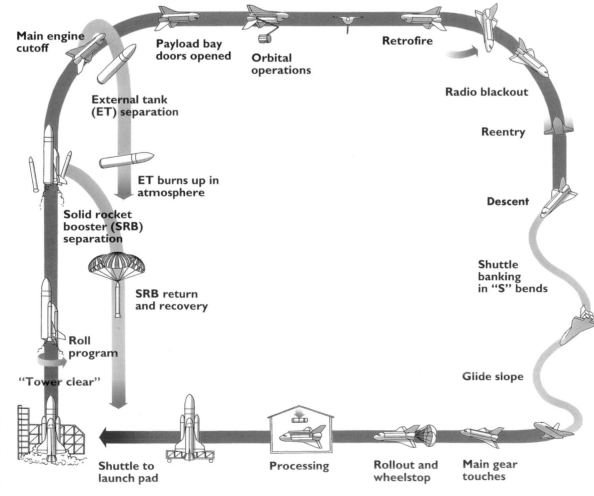

Main engine cutoff

Payload bay doors opened

Orbital operations

Retrofire

External tank (ET) separation

Radio blackout

Reentry

ET burns up in atmosphere

Descent

Solid rocket booster (SRB) separation

Shuttle banking in "S" bends

SRB return and recovery

Roll program

Glide slope

"Tower clear"

Shuttle to launch pad

Processing

Rollout and wheelstop

Main gear touches

The diagram on the left shows a typical NASA Space Shuttle mission profile, from countdown to touchdown and processing for the next mission. The Shuttle takes off from Kennedy Space Center, and ideally lands back there. Sometimes, for safety reasons, a landing is made in California. Then the orbiter has to be flown to KSC on a carrier aircraft (see page 16).

PARACHUTE DESCENT

After the intense heat of reentry is over, parachutes are released to slow the descent to Earth. NASA used to "splash-down" their spacecraft in the sea (1961-75), with a huge fleet of recovery ships and helicopters ready to pick up the astronauts. The Russians brought their cosmonauts to a land landing, or "dust-down," using a parachute and small retro-rockets to cushion the touchdown. This "dust-down" method is still used successfully by *Soyuz* reentry modules.

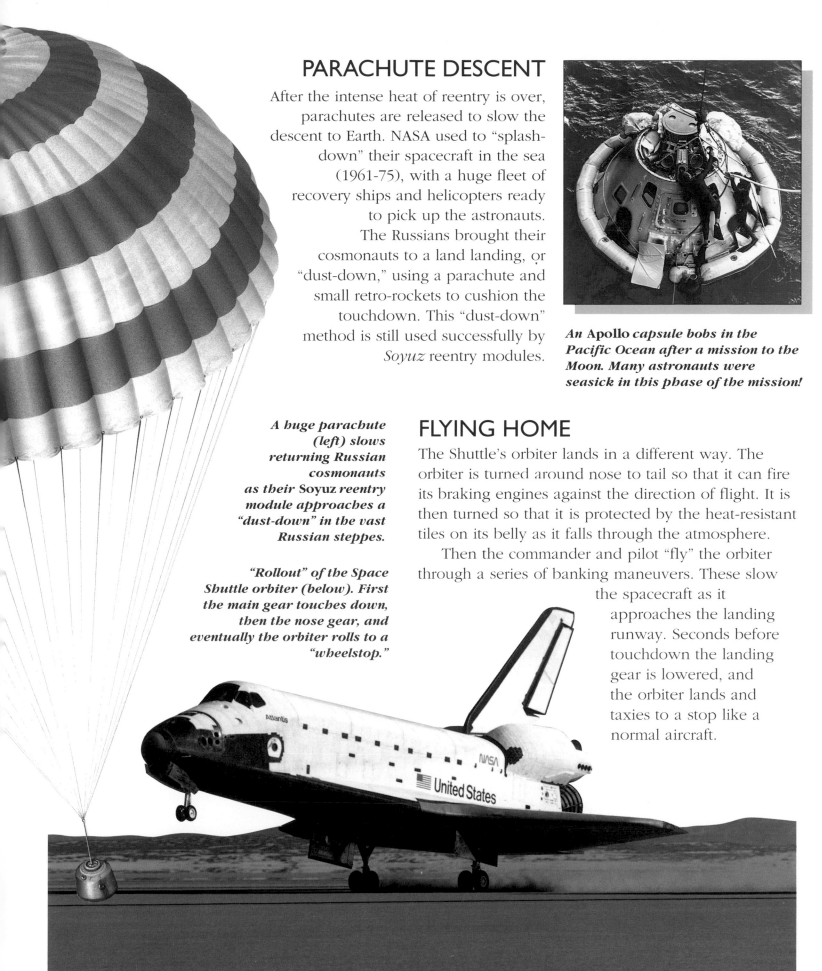

An Apollo *capsule bobs in the Pacific Ocean after a mission to the Moon. Many astronauts were seasick in this phase of the mission!*

A huge parachute (left) slows returning Russian cosmonauts as their Soyuz reentry module approaches a "dust-down" in the vast Russian steppes.

"Rollout" of the Space Shuttle orbiter (below). First the main gear touches down, then the nose gear, and eventually the orbiter rolls to a "wheelstop."

FLYING HOME

The Shuttle's orbiter lands in a different way. The orbiter is turned around nose to tail so that it can fire its braking engines against the direction of flight. It is then turned so that it is protected by the heat-resistant tiles on its belly as it falls through the atmosphere.

Then the commander and pilot "fly" the orbiter through a series of banking maneuvers. These slow the spacecraft as it approaches the landing runway. Seconds before touchdown the landing gear is lowered, and the orbiter lands and taxies to a stop like a normal aircraft.

GROUND CONTROL

All missions need the support of scientists, engineers, and technicians on Earth. The most famous are NASA's Mission Control Center in Houston, Texas, used for all U.S. manned space-flights, and the Jet Propulsion Laboratory in California, used for unmanned missions. In Russia, a huge center near Moscow controls the *Mir* space station.

GALILEO SPACE PROBE
"Dit-dit-dit-dit-dit" (digital data being transmitted to JPL Mission Control).

HUBBLE SPACE TELESCOPE
5. *"Blip blip, blip blip blip"* (signals being transmitted to user station).

MISSION CONTROL

In Mission Control, flight controllers monitor the mission around the clock. They check that the spacecraft is on the right course, that communications links are working, and that oxygen and fuel are not being used up too quickly. One astronaut, the capsule communicator ("CapCom"), is the link between the crew and Mission Control. At mission control, the Flight Director, ("Flight"), is responsible for the safety and success of the mission and crew.

DEEP SPACE

A less complex Mission Control is used for the unmanned deep-space probes. Good communications are essential for deep-space missions, because of the long distances to the spacecraft (it's nearly 62 million miles to Mars, for example). Signals must be directed very accurately at the spacecraft's antenna so that signals are received clearly. There are often many minutes of "silence" as the signal is traveling.

A Chinese mission control room. It seems very sparsely manned, compared to Russian and American mission controls.

DOMESTIC RELAY SATELLITE (DOMSAT)

Messages (right) are sent to spacecraft via the TDRS (Tracking & Data Relay Satellites). The TDRS ground station uses two main "bands" of electronic signals. The K band can send a lot of data quickly, but its beam is not easy to aim. The S band can't handle as much data, but its beam can be focused very accurately onto the antenna of a distant spacecraft.

JET PROPULSION LABORATORY, CALIFORNIA

MISSION CONTROL, HOUSTON, TEXAS
1. *"Discovery, this is Houston. Go for deploy."*

WHITE SANDS TRACKING STATION, NEW MEXICO
4. *"Houston - White Sands here. Signals received."*

DID YOU KNOW?

The design of computer on the Shuttle dates from the 1970s and has only 480 kilobytes of random access memory. (A modern home computer may have more than 2,000 kilobytes of RAM.) Many of the programs used on the mission are stored on tape and loaded into the main memory only when they are needed!

TRACKING & DATA RELAY SATELLITE (TDRS)

ASTRONAUT WITH CAMERA
3. *"This is Joe, TV view's fine from out here."*

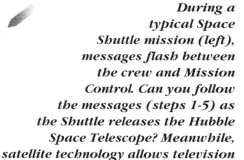

SPACE SHUTTLE DISCOVERY
2. *"Roger, Houston - this is Discovery - Copy your message. We have separation."*

During a typical Space Shuttle mission (left), messages flash between the crew and Mission Control. Can you follow the messages (steps 1-5) as the Shuttle releases the Hubble Space Telescope? Meanwhile, satellite technology allows television viewers to see events as they happen.

TRACKING

In the 1990s, missions are tracked by the Tracking & Data Relay Satellites (TDRS) deployed by the Shuttle. When deep-space manned flights are made, Mission Control will "talk" to the crews using the big dish antennas built for the *Apollo* and *Voyager* missions. The Russians have a fleet of tracking ships for monitoring their long-duration missions.

INTERNATIONAL RELAY SATELLITE (INTELSAT)

USER STATION

BBC TELEVISION, LONDON

HOME TELEVISION SET

SPACE SHUTTLE

Coming home. The intense heat seems to fold around the orbiter's nose.

Today, the most frequently used spacecraft is the NASA Space Shuttle. The Shuttle is launched like a rocket, flies like a spacecraft, and lands like a plane. It is a space truck, taking astronauts, cargo, and experiments into space, and returning satellites and equipment to Earth. The vehicle can be reused, flying many missions into Earth orbit.

ENGINES AND BOOSTERS

The main part of the Space Shuttle "stack" is the orbiter. It has three powerful main engines fueled from a large external tank. The external tank (ET) carries gallons of liquid hydrogen and oxygen. These liquids are mixed and ignited in the main engines to push the vehicle into space. After eight minutes the empty ET is discarded.

Two solid rocket boosters (SRBs) help launch the Shuttle. Once ignited they cannot be stopped until the solid fuel, a kind of sludge, is used up after about two minutes.

THE ORBITER

Shaped like an aircraft, the orbiter carries the crew and payload to and from space. It has wings and a tail for the landing phase. Maneuvering engines, located around the orbiter, can be fired up to change the craft's position in orbit.

As the Shuttle heads into orbit, its scorched external tank falls toward Earth. The ET, which is not reusable, will burn up in the Earth's atmosphere.

On the flightdeck in the 1980s. The countless controls of the 1970s-designed Shuttle now include lap-top computers and overhead displays.

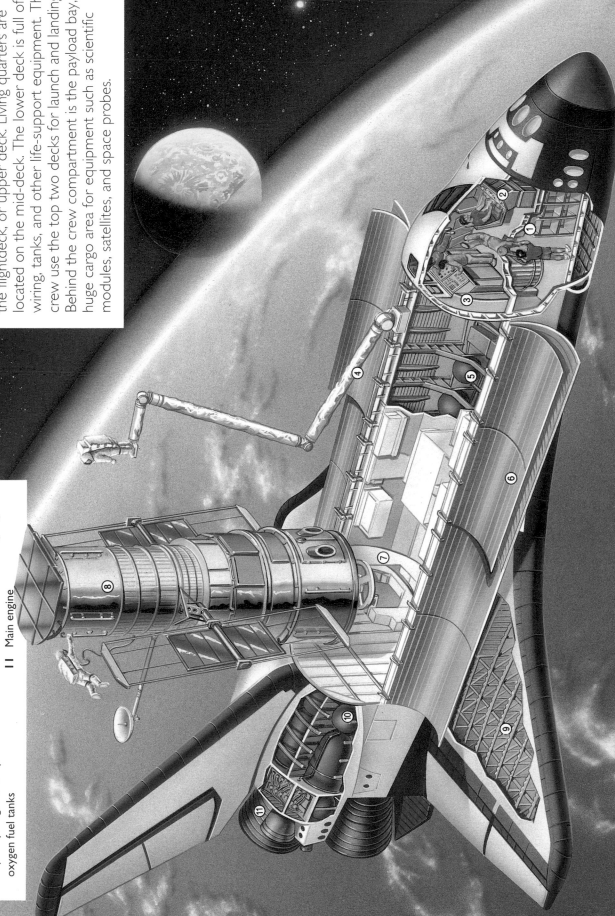

THE ORBITER

This is the Space Shuttle's orbiter, ready to repair the Hubble Space Telescope. The crew ride in the crew compartment at the front. This is divided into three sections. Flight and operations are controlled from the flightdeck, or upper deck. Living quarters are located on the mid-deck. The lower deck is full of wiring, tanks, and other life-support equipment. The crew use the top two decks for launch and landing. Behind the crew compartment is the payload bay, a huge cargo area for equipment such as scientific modules, satellites, and space probes.

REPAIRING HUBBLE

1 Crew compartment
2 Flight controls
3 Rear of flightdeck (with RMS controls)
4 Remote manipulator system (RMS)
5 Liquid hydrogen and liquid oxygen fuel tanks
6 Payload bay doors
7 Support deck for Hubble
8 Hubble Space Telescope
9 Wing ribs and tubular struts
10 Tanks for maneuvering engine
11 Main engine

ORBITAL OPERATIONS

As soon as the Shuttle is in orbit, the launch phase is completed. The payload bay doors are opened, and orbital operations – such as the deployment and retrieval of satellites and space probes – begin.

SATELLITE LAUNCHES

The Shuttle was designed as a commercial and military satellite launch system. Of the hundreds of satellites now orbiting the Earth, over 25 were launched by the Shuttle. Since 1984, Shuttle astronauts have retrieved several satellites for repair. This proved the advantage of the manned Shuttle over unmanned missions. Without astronauts, many repairs would not have been possible, and millions of dollars worth of satellites would have been lost.

PAYLOADS

The Shuttle is now used more for scientific research and launching space probes (see page 36). Probes and satellites are deployed from the bay using spring release mechanisms or, sometimes, a special robot arm, the remote manipulator system (RMS). The orbiter then moves away from the probe, which is fired on its way by a rocket called an inertial upper stage (IUS) booster.

Scientific missions use an additional Spacelab module. The orbiter can carry seven crew for 18 days in orbit.

Pressurized Spacelab module

Tunnel

The European Space Agency has developed the Spacelab scientific research module, which fits in the orbiter's payload bay.

The crew can move large objects using the RMS. They control the RMS from the aft (rear) flightdeck, looking into the payload bay. They can also see through TV cameras mounted on the arm. Sometimes the astronauts ride on the RMS (left). It's like standing on a diving board 125 miles high!

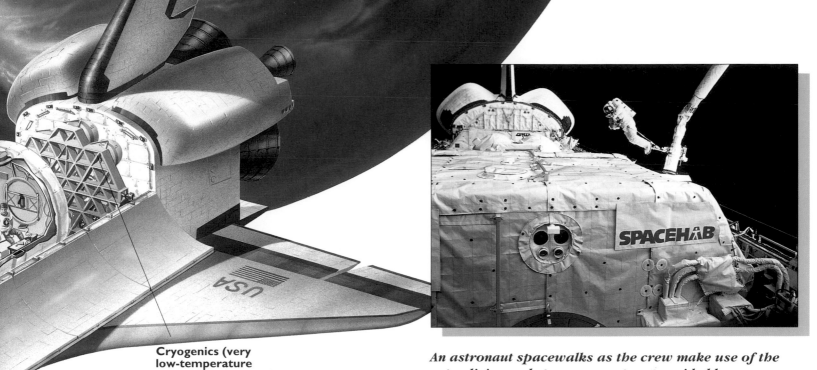

Cryogenics (very
low-temperature
storage) deck

*An astronaut spacewalks as the crew make use of the
extra living and storage quarters provided by a
Spacehab module. The astronaut is riding on the RMS.*

SPACEWALKS

Sometimes spacewalks are made
from the orbiter, in order to work
in the payload bay or retrieve
and repair satellites and orbiting
scientific equipment, such as the
Hubble Space Telescope (see
page 34). During the repair of a
communications satellite in 1991,
the astronauts were in their
spacesuits for over eight hours!
They could only take a few
drinks from their drink dispenser,
and they had to go to the toilet
using the suit's built-in toilet
system.

*An early Shuttle mission deploys a
commercial satellite (right).
Astronauts control the deployment
from the aft flightdeck, looking
through windows. When
the payload is
released, the
astronauts hear
a "clank"!*

LIFE IN SPACE

Joe Allen knows what it is like to fly in space. He made his first spaceflight in 1982 as a mission specialist on the Space Shuttle. Then, in 1985, he made a spacewalk to "capture" a faulty satellite for repair on Earth.

IN SPACE

"Just imagine floating in your own spaceship! Peering out, you watch the oceans and islands of Earth passing by your windows at breakneck speed. I nearly wrote '*below* your windows,' but in the weightless world of space your sense of 'up' is completely gone. You just float by the window and look at the scene moving past at five miles per second. Are *you* speeding by the continents, or are you just hovering in a magical gondola and watching the *world* turn beside you?"

All space explorers must exercise if they are to return to Earth in good condition. Treadmills, exercise bikes, and rowing machines have all been used by astronauts in space. On a recent Shuttle mission, this "bicycle" was cushioned on springs so that its vibrations didn't disturb sensitive scientific experiments.

The world spins by - Antarctica and Africa, as seen from Apollo 17 in 1972.

In space, it is easy to forget that objects float away if not held down. If astronauts lose something, they look for it near the air filters, where it might have been sucked by the air conditioning. One astronaut's watch was found four missions later!

AT WORK

Astronauts orbiting the Earth do not have a normal day and night as we do, so ship time for the crew is set to the time at Mission Control on Earth.

In orbit, the astronauts work in zero gravity. This makes it difficult to keep still when using equipment, so foot loops are provided. Outside the spacecraft, there are foot restraints for spacewalking astronauts, so they don't drift off into space. Spacecraft designers now ask astronauts to help design work benches, tools, and controls, to make their work more comfortable and productive.

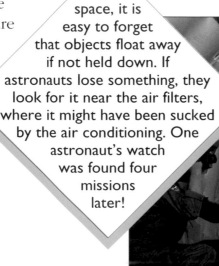

Astronauts wash using wet and dry towels. Here the "Vomit Comet" aircraft (see page 9) is being used to test a new "whole-body zero-g" shower.

Sleep stations or sleeping bags are provided for the crew (right). Scientific missions are usually completed by two shifts of astronauts, which allows two weeks' work on a one-week mission. Some astronauts are trying to sleep while others are working.

This is a typical food selection for astronauts (below). They also eat real fruit and M&M's. On Earth, our stomachs expand as we eat food. In weightless space, the astronauts' stomachs "float," and feel full all the time. However, most astronauts don't lose their appetite, so they still eat a healthy diet!

Astronauts' toothpaste is edible, and shaving foam is used with a safety razor to capture the whiskers. They use a vacuum to capture cut hair, and the air ducts for a blow dry!

WASTE DISPOSAL

Astronauts need to go to the toilet, of course. A spacecraft's toilet is usually worked by a vacuum system that sucks waste down into a reservoir. If the vacuum pump is too strong, the astronaut gets stuck to the seat. This is better than having too *weak* a seal, which lets waste seep out and float in mid-air! It is also better than the *Apollo* missions, when the astronauts had to go into a bag. The bag was sealed to the body with a strong sticky tape, which also pulled the hair from the astronaut's body!

◆ MADE IN SPACE

We have gone into space because the Universe is there, awaiting exploration and discovery. But have we benefited from the space program, despite the great cost? Going into space has broadened our understanding of life on Earth, and of the Universe where we live. And everyone on Earth has benefited from spin-offs from the space program.

MICROCHIPS

Only now, years after *Sputnik 1* was launched, is space research in everyone's homes. Today we take for granted the microchip technology in everything from watches to computers. Yet this was developed because engineers wanted to put lots of machines into the spacecraft. Existing computers were too big to fit into the small spacecraft and too heavy for the rockets to lift. Thus miniaturization and microchip computers had to be developed.

We benefit from a network of satellites in Earth orbit. This false-color satellite photo gives information about changes in sea levels. Satellites also enable us to see worldwide news events as they happen, and to monitor the weather, crop disease, and environmental damage.

The unmanned Long Duration Exposure Facility (LDEF) carried many experiments in Earth orbit. It was supposed to be retrieved in 1985, a year after its deployment. In fact, the Shuttle recaptured it in 1990!

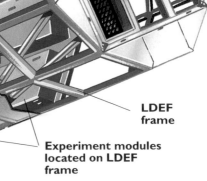

LDEF frame

Experiment modules located on LDEF frame

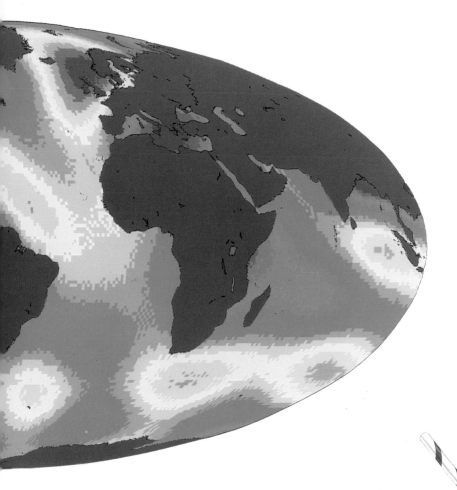

These space tomatoes were grown from seeds flown in the LDEF. They were part of an experiment to grow food from seeds exposed to spaceflight conditions.

MEDICAL DEVELOPMENTS

Some dramatic advances in space research have found their way into hospitals on Earth. Micro- and plastic surgery have benefited from the space program. And surgeons now use a form of the spacesuit for protection and cleanliness.

Experiments have produced medicines in space. Because of the lack of gravity, these medicines will be purer than ones made on Earth. Surgery in orbit is still some way off, though. One major problem is getting the patient safely to and from orbit!

Space technology has found its way into homes on Earth - including methods of preserving and storing food, such as airproof soda cans!

Foil drink container with straw

Calculator with LED display

Aluminum foil

Computer chips

Perfectly round ball bearings

Velcro

Watch with LED display

Soda can

Mobile phone

INDUSTRY

Production of industrial parts in space is another new technology. For example, a ball bearing made on Earth is affected by gravity, so it is not perfectly spherical. In space, there's no gravity, so a truly perfect sphere is formed. This ball bearing will work more smoothly, and it and the machine it is in will last longer.

SPACESUITS

The extra-vehicular activity (EVA) spacesuit is a mini spacecraft. It provides the oxygen, heating, cooling, communication, refreshment, and toilet facilities an astronaut needs to work outside the spacecraft. Astronaut Joe Allen describes how he "suited up" in the Space Shuttle:

BUNDLED UP

"Putting on the EVA spacesuit always reminded me of when my mother dressed me in a very heavy snowsuit. In this case, your shipmates bundle you up. They stuff you in the spacesuit, often with a pat on the back and a butter cookie in the mouth for good luck. Then they put the helmet over your head, snap it into place, and from that moment on *you float in the suit*, your head occasionally bobbing up against the helmet.

"You are now floating in a space-age cocoon, and because of its protection you can float right out through the hatch. Using the controls of a Manned Maneuvering Unit (MMU), you can even move yourself away from the mother ship. You are then orbiting the Earth as surely as the Moon orbits the Earth, and you are a satellite!"

A crew walks out to the Shuttle. Their bulging pockets are full of items such as gloves, mission data files, and sandwiches (in case there's a delay in launching). The basic Shuttle coverall suits and helmets (which have already been placed in the Shuttle) will protect the crew if cabin oxygen is lost during lift-off.

EVA suits must be packed for storage in the airlock (right).

Every spacesuit is tested before each mission. Below, an EVA suit's pressure and electronics are being checked.

On *Apollo 16*, astronaut Charlie Duke was taller due to the lack of gravity, and had difficulty getting into his spacesuit. He also got a surprise on a moon walk when his in-suit drink dispenser failed - it gave his hair an orange-juice shampoo!

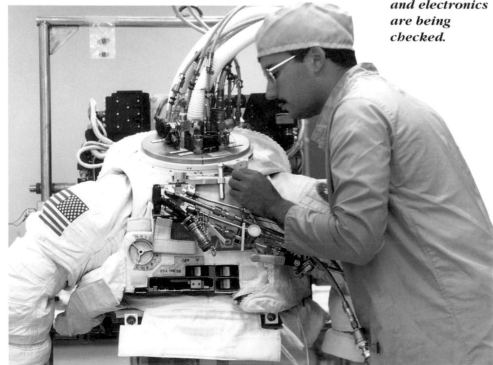

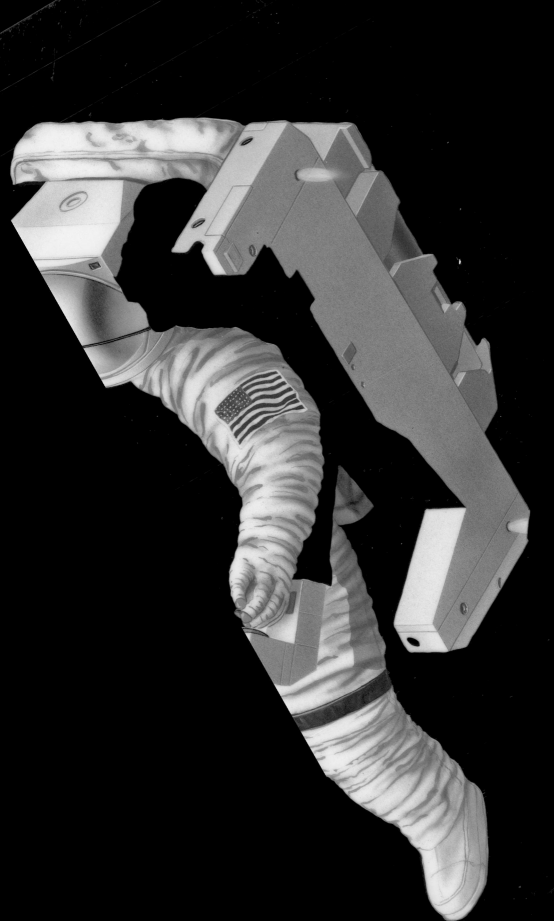

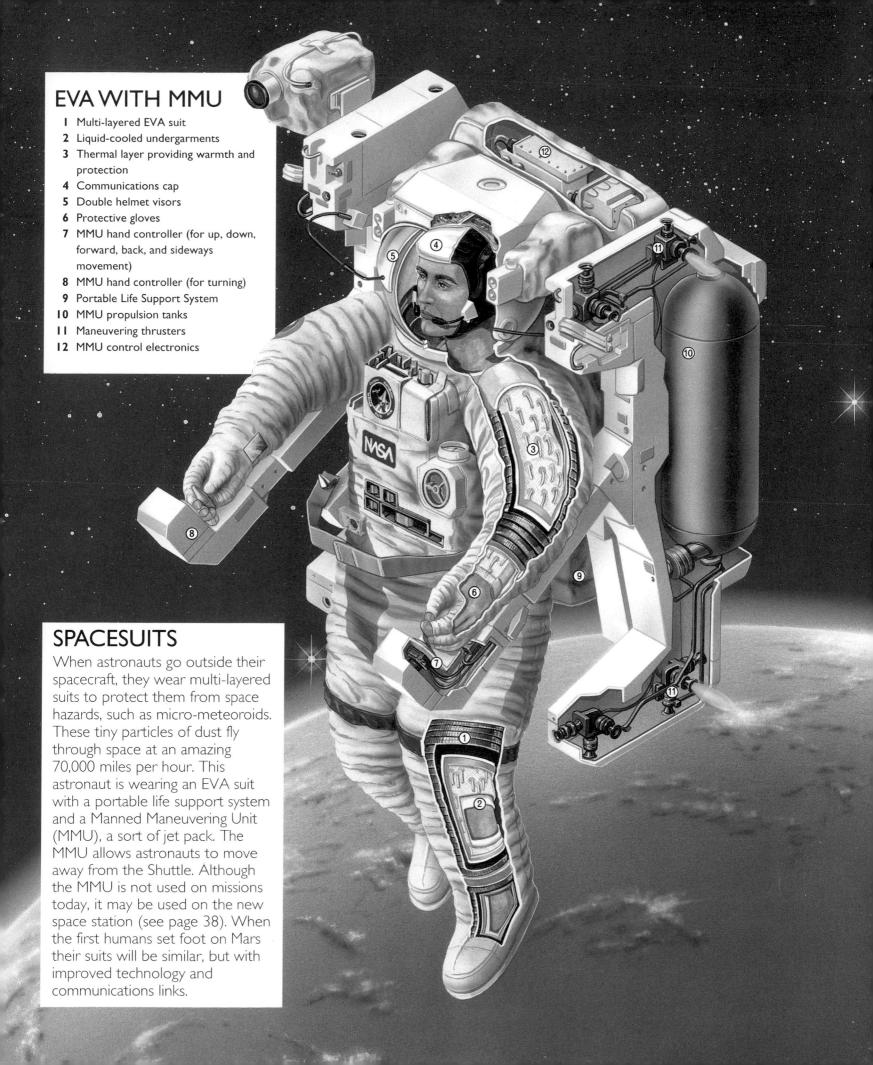

EVA WITH MMU

1 Multi-layered EVA suit
2 Liquid-cooled undergarments
3 Thermal layer providing warmth and
   protection
4 Communications cap
5 Double helmet visors
6 Protective gloves
7 MMU hand controller (for up, down,
   forward, back, and sideways
   movement)
8 MMU hand controller (for turning)
9 Portable Life Support System
10 MMU propulsion tanks
11 Maneuvering thrusters
12 MMU control electronics

SPACESUITS

When astronauts go outside their
spacecraft, they wear multi-layered
suits to protect them from space
hazards, such as micro-meteoroids.
These tiny particles of dust fly
through space at an amazing
70,000 miles per hour. This
astronaut is wearing an EVA suit
with a portable life support system
and a Manned Maneuvering Unit
(MMU), a sort of jet pack. The
MMU allows astronauts to move
away from the Shuttle. Although
the MMU is not used on missions
today, it may be used on the new
space station (see page 38). When
the first humans set foot on Mars
their suits will be similar, but with
improved technology and
communications links.

EYE IN THE SKY

The deployment of the Hubble Space Telescope in 1990 was a huge advance in space exploration. Over 370 miles above the Earth's atmosphere, Hubble would have a clear view of the Universe. It would also be able to "see" types of radiation that are absorbed by the atmosphere before they reach telescopes on Earth.

HUBBLE TROUBLE

Unfortunately, Hubble didn't work properly. There were problems with its huge mirror system, which blurred the telescope's sight! Fortunately, using new computer techniques, scientists were still able to detect more stars in space, and calculate their age and distance much more accurately. Eventually, the Shuttle astronauts were sent up to adjust the mirrors. They also replaced the telescope's solar panels, which were wearing out. Hubble is now working much better.

Antenna

Solar panel

Secondary mirror assembly

Main mirror assembly

Hubble's many instruments can plot the position of distant galaxies and observe the detailed structures of galaxies and planets . . .

detect and capture images of faint and distant objects . . .

The Hubble Space Telescope.

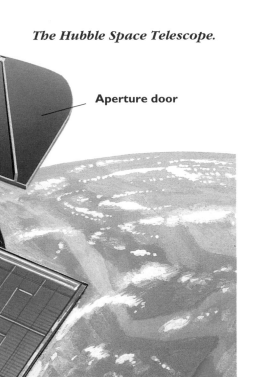

Aperture door

ORBITING OBSERVATORIES

Hubble is one of several large observatories in orbit. When it is working properly, Hubble can see objects that are 50 times fainter and 7 times farther away than any objects a telescope on Earth can see. Information from Hubble and other space observatories, such as the Compton Gamma Ray Observatory, will teach us more about our Universe and help plan future missions and experiments.

The Compton Gamma Ray Observatory (above) is studying faint sources of gamma rays in the Universe.

The Earth's atmosphere is struck by a wide range of rays and particles (below). Only visible light, infrared, and radio waves actually reach the ground and can be observed by ground telescopes.

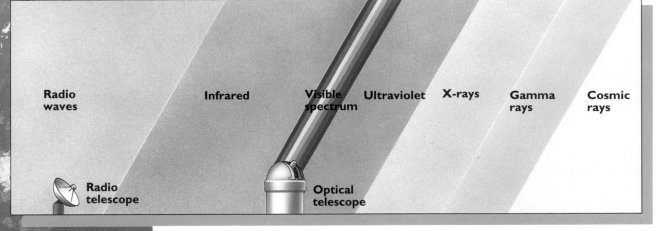

Radio waves   Infrared   Visible spectrum   Ultraviolet   X-rays   Gamma rays   Cosmic rays

Radio telescope   Optical telescope

detect and measure the light waves of faint objects . . .   *and track and map the position of stars.*

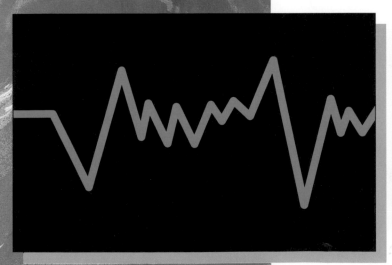

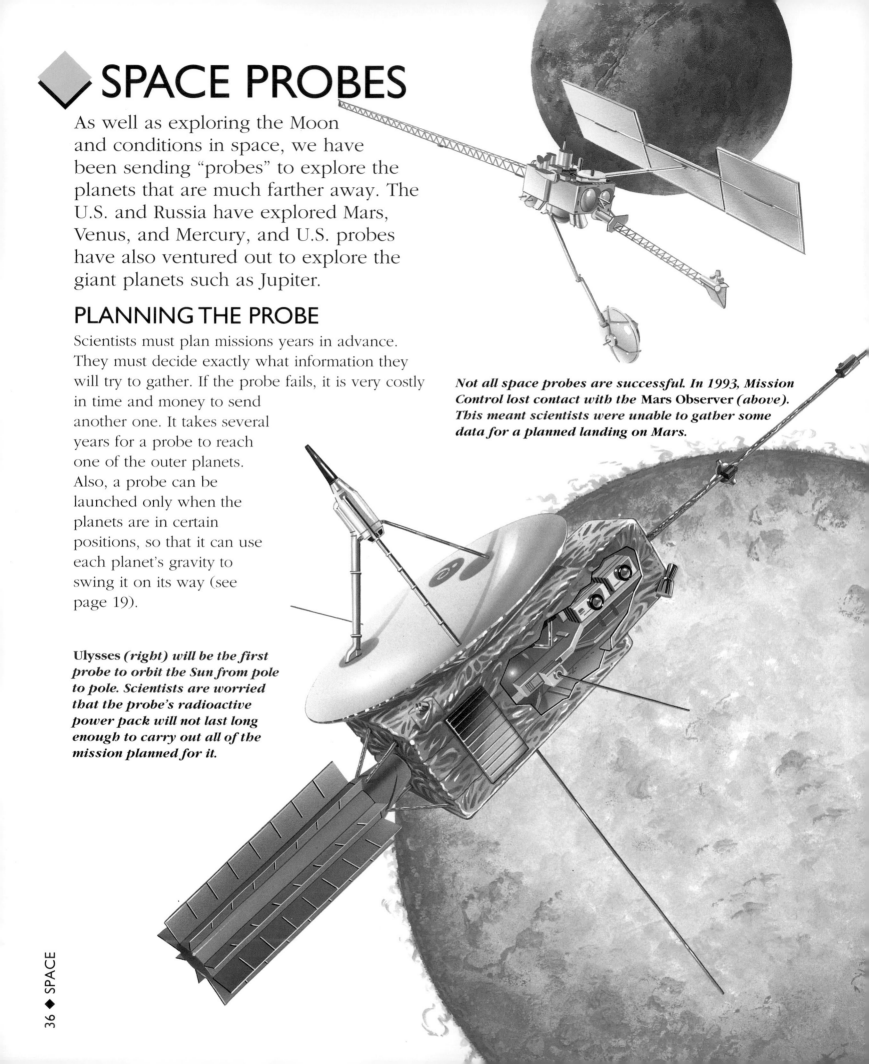

SPACE PROBES

As well as exploring the Moon and conditions in space, we have been sending "probes" to explore the planets that are much farther away. The U.S. and Russia have explored Mars, Venus, and Mercury, and U.S. probes have also ventured out to explore the giant planets such as Jupiter.

PLANNING THE PROBE

Scientists must plan missions years in advance. They must decide exactly what information they will try to gather. If the probe fails, it is very costly in time and money to send another one. It takes several years for a probe to reach one of the outer planets. Also, a probe can be launched only when the planets are in certain positions, so that it can use each planet's gravity to swing it on its way (see page 19).

Not all space probes are successful. In 1993, Mission Control lost contact with the Mars Observer (above). This meant scientists were unable to gather some data for a planned landing on Mars.

Ulysses (right) will be the first probe to orbit the Sun from pole to pole. Scientists are worried that the probe's radioactive power pack will not last long enough to carry out all of the mission planned for it.

THE GIANT PLANETS

The first deep-space probes were *Pioneer 10* and *11* in the 1970s, but it was the two *Voyager* probes that finally gave spectacular views of Jupiter, Saturn, Neptune, and Uranus. They successfully used the "slingshot" technique (see page 18) to travel to the edge of the solar system.

Space probe *Galileo* (see page 18) will soon release a probe into Jupiter's atmosphere, and *Magellan*'s radar has recently scanned Venus.

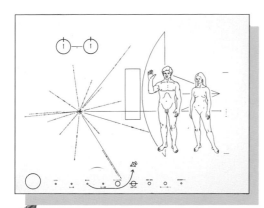

After having flown by Jupiter, Pioneer 10 and 11 passed into deep space. In case the probes are found by another advanced civilization, scientists attached this plaque telling the "aliens" about the Earth and its life.

OTHER TARGETS

The planets are not the only targets for probes. The *Ulysses* probe is now heading through space to observe both poles of the Sun, our nearest star. However, it will be many years before a probe could possibly reach another star. The distances are so enormous that it would be very difficult to communicate with the probe, and to give it a power supply that will last for such a long time.

TV camera and spectrometer

Thrusters

Antenna

Fuel tank

Extendable boom

Magnetometer (for detecting magnetic fields)

Radioactive thermoelectric generators

There have been many space probes launched to explore our solar system. Here are some important ones, with their dates of launch.

Mariner IV	USA	11/64	Photographed Mars
Venera 4	USSR	06/67	Sent data on Venus's atmosphere
Venera 7	USSR	08/70	Sent data from Venus's surface
Mariner IX	USA	05/71	First probe to orbit Mars
Pioneer 10	USA	02/72	Flew past Jupiter. Became first spacecraft to pass all outer planets. Now 5.6 billion miles from the Sun
Pioneer-Saturn	USA	04/73	Flew past Saturn
Mariner X	USA	11/73	First probe to fly by two planets: Venus and Mercury
Voyager 2	USA	08/77	Flew past Jupiter, Saturn, Uranus, and Neptune
Voyager 1	USA	09/77	Flew past Jupiter and Saturn
Giotto	Europe	07/85	Flew past Halley's Comet. Discovered center of comet is an icy ball containing organic compounds

The Voyager probes (above) have now left our solar system. Voyager 1 is more than 5 billion miles from the Sun - that's nearly 50 times farther away from the Sun than the Earth is.

SPACE STATIONS

A space station is an ideal base from which an astronaut can prepare for exploring space and conducting scientific experiments. As with most ideas about spaceflight, the idea of space stations could be found in books long before the first satellite flew.

SCIENCE FICTION - SCIENCE FACT

Science fiction space stations are always huge, complex designs, almost as large as a small city on Earth. But the first space stations were little more than the size of a house. The American 100-ton *Skylab* was a converted moon rocket stage, and the Russian *Salyut* had an interior about the size of a subway train car.

These first small space stations carried out valuable research, but bigger stations that would last for much longer were needed. Therefore the *Salyut* stations became part of the *Mir* space complex (see page 41). The largest space station plans are for the U.S. international program.

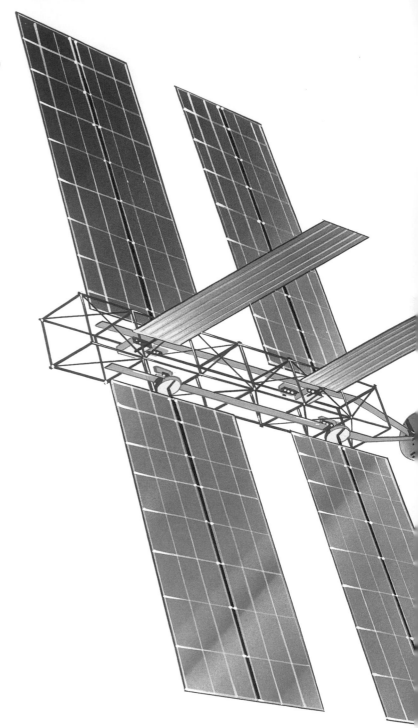

The first U.S. space station, **Skylab,** *is seen orbiting with one solar wing (below). Its other wing was lost during launch. Three teams of three astronauts spent 28, 59, and 84 days respectively in this former* **Saturn V** *moon rocket stage.* **Skylab** *eventually dropped into Earth's atmosphere. In 1979 it burned up and scattered debris across Australia.*

A NEW INTERNATIONAL STATION

The design and name of the new station has changed over the years, as the cost of the program has increased. The basic station consists of a group of modules linked together and powered by solar panels. Countries and space agencies from around the world will provide different elements of the station.

This large complex is expected to remain in orbit for up to 30 years. It will probably be commanded by a scientist, and its crew will include people from many nations.

RESEARCH AND EXPERIMENTS

The space station's research will concentrate on life sciences and medical experiments. For example, studying the effects of weightlessness on the body is of importance for long spaceflights to planets such as Mars. Research into materials and observations of the Earth will be another important part of the work. The station will eventually be a base for manned exploration of the Moon and Mars.

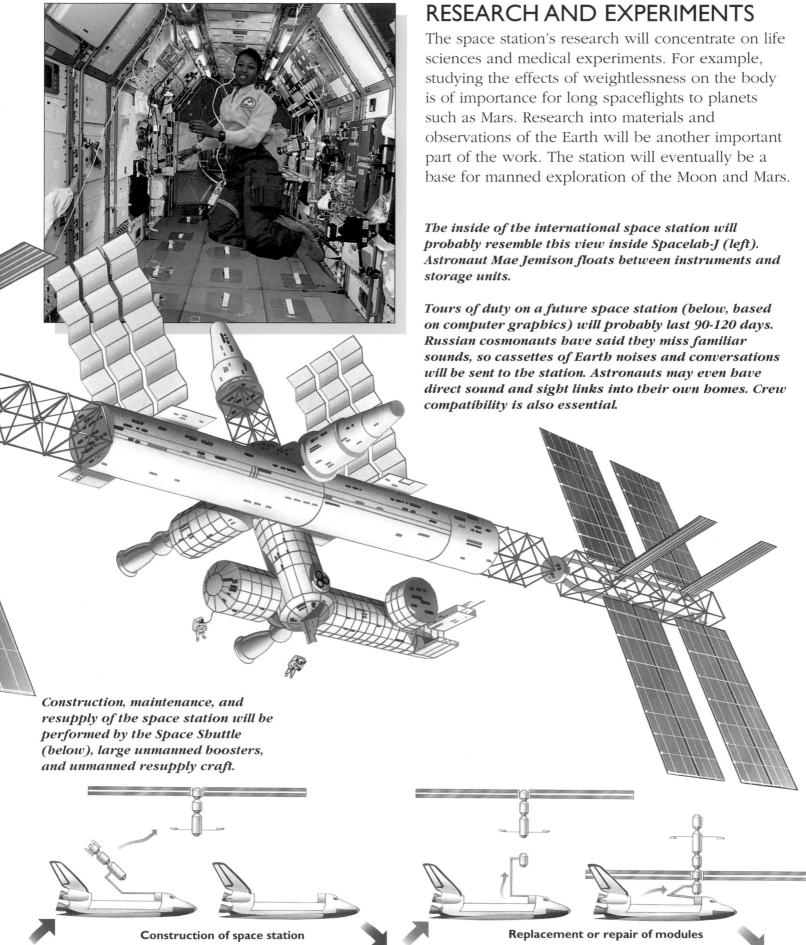

The inside of the international space station will probably resemble this view inside Spacelab-J (left). Astronaut Mae Jemison floats between instruments and storage units.

Tours of duty on a future space station (below, based on computer graphics) will probably last 90-120 days. Russian cosmonauts have said they miss familiar sounds, so cassettes of Earth noises and conversations will be sent to the station. Astronauts may even have direct sound and sight links into their own homes. Crew compatibility is also essential.

Construction, maintenance, and resupply of the space station will be performed by the Space Shuttle (below), large unmanned boosters, and unmanned resupply craft.

Construction of space station

Replacement or repair of modules

SPACE STATION *MIR*

In February 1986 the Soviet Union launched the first section of a new space station. The station, called *Mir*, is made up of several modules that are taken into space and then joined together.

A HOME IN SPACE

The main module contains only the crew quarters, flight controls, and exercise equipment. Because they spend about six months in the zero gravity of space, the crew use the station's mini-gym regularly so their muscles do not waste away. The crew return to Earth in a *Soyuz* spacecraft.

The first add-on section, called *Kvant-1*, was attached in 1987. It carried x-ray telescopes for studying a supernova, a rapidly brightening star.

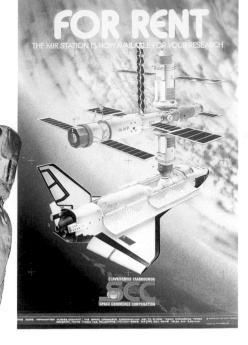

*"For Rent." To help cover the costs of **Mir**, the Soviet space agency sold space for scientific experiments and flights for foreign cosmonauts.*

*When Kvant-2 was docked to **Mir**, it took with it a manned maneuvering unit called **Ickarus**. This MMU has enabled the cosmonauts to carry out repair work in space.*

SCIENTIFIC EQUIPMENT

The main scientific equipment was to be added in four additional modules. The first, *Kvant-2*, was attached to *Mir* in December 1989. The last module docked, *Kristall*, has a large furnace for making metals in zero gravity.

The next modules, *Spectr* and *Priroda*, will study the Earth's natural resources and observe its atmosphere. They were designed to be taken up by the new Russian space shuttle *Buran*. It is more likely they will be sent up on unmanned launchers or the U.S. Space Shuttle.

THE FUTURE OF *MIR*

There were also plans to attach a medical lab to *Mir*. However, because of its cost, the future of *Mir* is increasingly dependent on international assistance, but plans for a *Mir 2* continue.

*There's very little room for the cosmonauts in **Mir**, or in the **Soyuz** spacecraft (above), which takes them to and from the station. **Mir** itself is full of equipment and cluttered with the cosmonauts' personal items, such as music cassettes.*

THE MIR ACHIEVEMENT

Mir is a magnificent achievement. It weighs 800 tons - without *Spectr* and *Priroda* - and generates its electricity from a huge array of solar panels. The top scene shows *Mir* with *Kvant-2* and *Kristall* added, and a *Soyuz* spacecraft approaching. The lower picture shows *Soyuz* and the other modules docked to the main docking unit.

THE MIR COMPLEX

1 *Progress* resupply vehicle	6 Telescopic solar panel
2 *Kvant-1* astronomy module	7 *Kvant-2* module
3 Cosmonaut using MMU	8 *Priroda* module
4 Central docking unit for modules	9 *Spectr* module
5 *Mir* main module	10 *Soyuz TM* spacecraft
	11 *Kristall* space factory
	12 Docking unit

TO THE PLANETS

In the early part of the next century, manned flight to Mars will be a real possibility. Mars is the closest planet to Earth that humans are capable of exploring. There are also advanced plans to establish a research base on the Moon.

BASES ON THE SURFACE

Plans for the exploration of Mars have existed for many years: only the funds to pay for such an expensive trip are needed. The first human explorers of Mars will be scientific researchers gathering as much information on their new environment as they can, in the same way explorers did in the first South Pole bases.

Simulations of Mars bases are now being developed. Isolation experiments have existed in the Soviet Union since the 1960s, and the U.S.'s *Biosphere 2* is a prototype of a future closed ecological system that might, one day, sit on the surface of Mars. Because of the huge distance to Mars (a two-year round trip compared to a week to the Moon and back), the explorers will stay on its surface for several weeks during each expedition.

Mars was visited by both American and Soviet unmanned missions in the 1960s and 1970s. The American **Mariner** *series of spacecraft took outstanding photos of Mars. These pictures were used to plan exploration in 1976 by two* **Viking** *spacecraft (above), which also carried orbiting vehicles.*

MARS AND BEYOND

If people are born in the low gravity of the Moon or Mars, they might not be able to withstand the the Earth's stronger gravity. They might have to remain on Mars forever!

With Mars colonized and large bases on the Moon and in Earth orbit, the next target would probably be the asteroids for major mining operations.

Jul   *Apollo 15* astronauts drive first car, the Lunar Rover, on Moon.

1973
May   American *Skylab* space station launched.

1975
Jul   American astronauts and Soviet cosmonauts meet and shake hands in orbit during joint ASTP mission.

1976
Jul   *Viking 1* soft lands on Mars, followed in September by *Viking 2.*

1977
Sep   Soviet space station *Salyut 6* launched, followed in 1982 by *Salyut 7*, paving way for *Mir* space station.

1979
Mar   *Voyager 1* flies within 177,000 miles of Jupiter's cloud tops.

Dec   First European *Ariane* rocket launched.

1981
Apr   *Columbia*, the first NASA Space Shuttle, launched into space.

1983
Jul   *Pioneer 10* is first probe to pass Pluto, the outer planet of the solar system.

1986
Jan   *Voyager 2* passes Uranus. Space Shuttle *Challenger* explodes 73 seconds after launch, killing crew of seven.

Feb   *Mir* space station launched.

1988
Dec   Cosmonauts Titov and Manarov return to Earth after record flight of 366 days 18 hours 7 minutes - the first "year" in orbit.

1989
Oct   *Galileo* deployed for voyage to Jupiter.

1993
Dec   Hubble Space Telescope repaired.

Moments from the exploration of space (below). From left to right: Sketches by Konstantin Tsiolkovsky circa 1900. A U.S. A-4 rocket (a captured German V-2) is launched in 1946. Lunokhod 2 and Luna 21 explore the Moon in 1973. The Space Shuttle orbiter Enterprise separates from its Boeing 747 carrier aircraft for a test flight in 1977. A Mars Shuttle flies between planets, and the first landing by humans on Mars, in the 21st century.

INDEX

A-4 rocket 47
Aldrin, "Buzz" 11, 46
Allen, Joe 2, 28, 32
Apollo program 10-11, 28-29, 45, 46, 47
Ariane rocket 13, 14, 47
Aristarchus 4
Armstrong, Neil 7, 11, 46
Atlantis shuttle 14

Baikonur Cosmodrome 14
ballistic rockets 7, 13
Biosphere 2 42
Buran shuttle 40

Challenger
    lunar module 11
    Space Shuttle 47
Collins, Michael 11
Columbia shuttle 47
command module 11, 17
communications satellite 27, 46
Compton Gamma Ray Observatory 35
Copernicus 4
countdown 17, 20

Delta Clipper 44
Duke, Charlie 32

Enterprise shuttle 47
European Space Agency 26
Explorer satellite 7, 46
external tanks (ETs) 13, 24
extra-vehicular activity suit 32-33, 41

flightdeck 24-25, 26
Flight Director 22
flight path 18
flight plan 8

Gagarin, Yuri 8-9, 14, 46
Galileo, Galilei 4-5
Galileo probe 18-19, 22, 37, 47
Gemini-Titan rocket 12
G-forces 16
Giotto probe 37
Goddard, Robert 6, 7
gravity 11, 42
    escape 13, 18
    slingshot 18-19, 36-37
ground control 16, 22-23
H-II launcher 13
Halley's Comet 4, 37
heat shield 20
Hermes shuttle 45
Hubble Space Telescope 22, 34-35
    repair 25, 27, 47

Ickarus MMU 40
inertial upper stage (IUS) booster 26

Jemison, Mae 39
jet engines 13
Jet Propulsion Laboratory 22
Jupiter 4
    manned flights 43

probes 18-19, 36-37, 47

Kennedy, President John F. 10, 46
Kennedy Space Center (KSC) 14, 16, 20
Kepler 4

launch 14, 15, 16-17, 18
    vehicles 12-13
Leonov, Alexei 46
light years 5
Long Duration Exposure Facility 30
Luna probes 10-11, 46, 47
Lunar Rover 11, 47

Magellan probe 37
Manarov 47
Manned Maneuvering Unit (MMU) 32-33,
    40, 41
Mariner probes 37, 42, 46
Mars 5, 22
    base 8, 42
    landings 33, 47
    probes 36-37, 46
Mercury 4, 36-37
Mercury-Atlas rocket 12
Mercury capsule 8
Mir space station 22, 38, 40-41, 47
Mission Control 22-23, 36
Moon 4, 5
    base 8, 42-43
    missions 10-11, 45
    vehicles 47
    walk 11, 46
multi-axial trainer 8
Muses-A 10

NASA 20, 24, 46
    Mission Control 22
navigation 18
Neptune 5, 37, 43
Newton 4

Oberth, Hermann 6
orbiter, Shuttle 24-27, 47
    launch 13, 16
    reentry 20-21

payload bay 20, 25, 26-27
payloads 13, 15, 18-19
Pioneer probes 37, 47
planets 4-5, 34
    manned flights 42-43
    probes 36
Pluto 4, 47
portable life support system (PLSS) 33
probes 10-11, 26, 36-37

Ranger 7 10
reentry 20-21
relay satellites 22-23
remote manipulator system (RMS) 26, 27
rockets 6-7, 12-13

Salyut space station 3, 47
satellites 30
    communications 27, 46
    first 6-7, 46
    launch and retrieval 26, 27

relay 22-23
research 35
weather 46
Saturn 4, 37, 43
Saturn rockets 12-13
Schmitt, Jack 11
Shepard, Alan 46
Single Stage to Orbit (SSTO) vehicle 44
Skylab 38, 47
solar panels 34, 38, 41
solar system 4-5, 37, 47
solid rocket boosters (SRBs) 13, 20, 24
Soyuz 40, 41, 46
    cosmonauts 15
    launch 17
    reentry 21
    SL-4 12, 17
Spacelab 26, 39
spacesuits 27, 29, 32-33
    future 44
Space Shuttle 12, 24-25, 28
    Atlantis 14
    Columbia 47
    launch 16
    navigation 18
    orbiter 13, 16, 26-27, 47
    return 6, 20-21
    space station 39, 40
    spacesuits 32
space stations 33, 38-39, 47
    Mir 22, 38, 40-41, 47
space technology 30-31
Space Transportation System 12
    see also Space Shuttle
spacewalks 17, 28, 46
"splash-down" 21
Sputnik satellites 6-7, 30, 46
Sun 4-5, 18, 19
    probes 36-37
Surveyor 3 mission 10

telescopes 5, 34-35, 40
Telstar 1 satellite 46
Tereshkova, Valentina 46
thrusters 19, 37
Titov 47
touchdown 20-21
Tsiolkovsky, Konstantin 4, 47

Uranus 4, 37, 43, 47

V-2 rocket 47
Vanguard satellite 7, 46
Verne, Jules 7
Venera probes 37
Venus 4, 18
    probes 36, 37
Viking probes 42, 47
Vostok 1 8, 9
Voyager missions 23, 37, 47

weather satellite 46
weightlessness 28, 39

zero gravity 8, 9, 27
    exercise in 40
    living in 28-29
    Spacelab 39

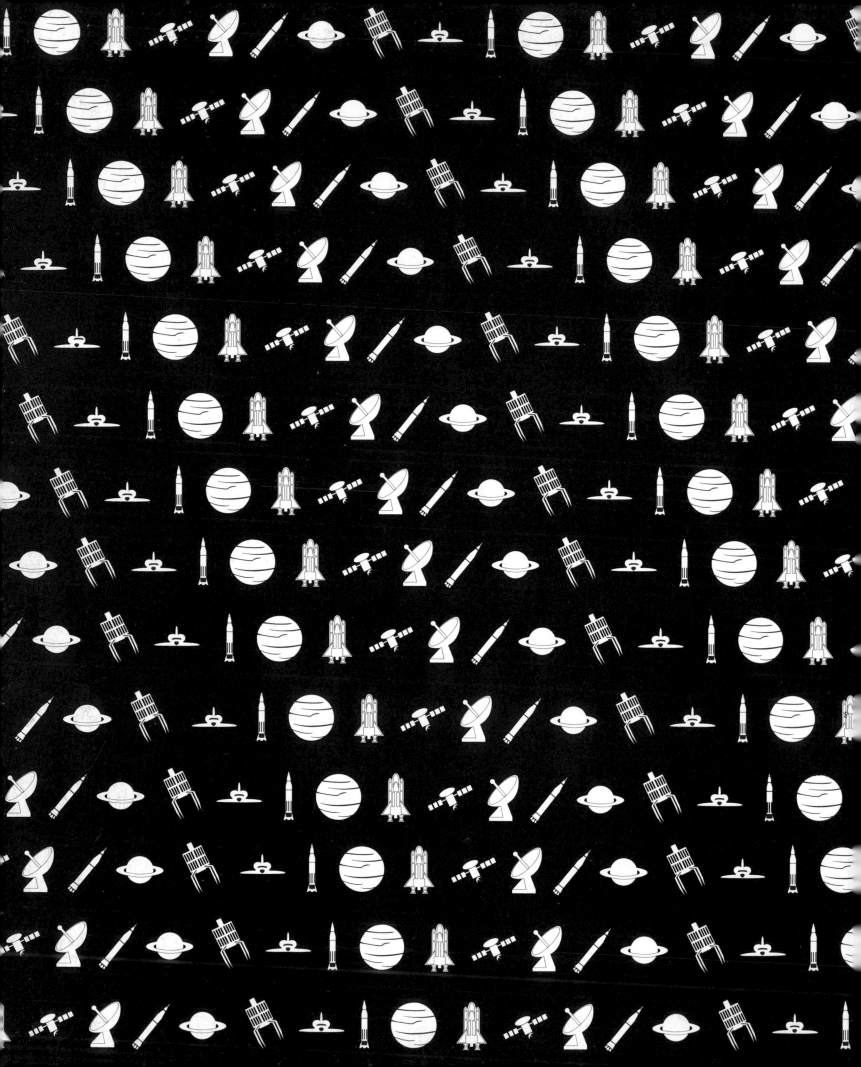